Introspection

Rim Darras

BookLeaf Publishing

Presentation by *BookLeaf Publishing*

Web: www.bookleafpub.com

E-mail: info@bookleafpub.com

ISBN: 978-93-95755-82-5

First edition 2022

To Lalla, my grandmother.

Forever the embodiment of Home.

I miss you dearly and love you always..

PREFACE

I feel like every profound reflection, either starts with or leads to introspection. It is the unavoidable path to an honest conversation within oneself. Whether it is healing, confusing, joyful, or distressing, the result is often a purge and a calmer mind. And as we try to address ourselves, our real selves deep inside, and shake the habit of pretending, we might stumble upon the beauty of it all, ours, and our world's, and make a habit of introspecting.

The shadow of the Moon

It was one of those nights

Where the darkness spilled its velvety body

All over the restless town

Where the silver moon mocked us all

With the snide shimmering

Of its pearly crescent

Where even the stars' dusty glimmers

Laid their web, as to trap our spirits

It was one of those nights

Where the sky felt too heavy for our tired
shoulders…

Sincerity

2

Sincerity is lost

In a world without words…but with too much to say

Sincerity is lost

With so many silenced voices…drowning in a deafening cry

Sincerity is lost

When millions lie mute…in a sea of indifferent cacophony

Sincerity is l o s…t

When we count our characters to share…but let our sharing character die

Awake

The machine's blue light
Drowned my tired face
My eyes squinted into two fine lines
Deciphering the cabalistic signs floating in front of
me
Black crows on the luminescent white screen
The night was dripping, bottomless and dark
My feet were submerged in it, feeling its chilling
breeze
Time stretched into infinity
Glass, plastic, and carbon, as cold as the dreadful
evening
Rubbing against my palms, meeting my fingertips
Were as needles and pins
Under my burning skin
Amidst the deafening silence
Sliced by the humming unit
Only spoke my livid reflection
On the monitor, with eyes sleepless
And fever draining from every pore

Mourning

Mourning all the conversations
I won't get to have anywhere other than in my mind,
Those swift verbal variations
Phrasing nuances and clever wording of a different
kind
Why do they only flourish foolishly wild
Lilac Asters, orange Poppy and Marigolds Oh so
yellow!
Within the closed chambers of my thoughts, by
design
Starburst of color, waves of carefully crafted lines,
meadow
A proud and plentiful land with no one to feed
When my reason wanders and rebels, defiant steed
But prisoner it is, of an unscalable wall
Of circumstances, fears, anxious sprawl
And those glorious, lustrous dreams
Where I dazzle with intellect, prowess, sagacity
And good nature, and beam!
All autumn leaves swept by the winds of reality…

Anxious

That burning sensation
Belly aching and torn
By a lingering defeat
I dread the dawn, its thorns
And the livid light
Brought up by the day starting
White fear sweating from the windows
Seeping from every interstice
Threatens to drown all hope
In its milky throat
While I stare at the snowy ceiling
As colorless as my resolve
To leave my bed this pale morning

Spark

6

Saw a glimmering light
Once, nestling in the dark
And its flickering gleam, despite
Floating in a sea of Black
Cast a wave of warmth, quite
A beacon, a shimmer, a spark
As if swallowing the night
Comforted my sorrowful heart

Depression

Sleepless doubts budding in the air
Metallic taste of a violent aversion
Nervous tension slicing through the atmosphere
Braving the bold daylight with dark subversion
The Lead-footed giant took ominous shape
In the smoky space floating in the room
Made of the ill-spirited moxie, in desolation draped
He towered over the bed, creature of gloom
All seemed lost in the hopeless stillness
As the day soaked in a somber anguish
And the weariness took hold, silent witness
Of the tribulations the mind couldn't vanquish

Missing you/I'll find you

I'll find you
In a homemade meal
In that color between blue and teal
In old French lullabies
In pictures, in memories, in cries

I'll find you
In prayers and aged tunes alike
In a florid lightning strike
In the sound waterfalls make
In a timeworn, white-powdered keepsake

I'll find you
In the depths of my heart
At my every thought and affection start
In my tenderest, sweetest dreams
In the whispering wind, the feathery sky, and the untouched streams

And in whatever reality or unfolded scheme
I'll find you…

Heart all mine

I have caged it
My heart,
So that no other would
I padded it
With lies,
Carefully crafted falsehood
I hid it
So deep,
In a boundless schism
I made it
Seem bleak,
Gray void in a colorless prism
I tucked it
Away,
Like stars under the day's husk
After a while
It may,
Fade into the cool tangerine dusk
But no matter,
It will,
Escape heartache and anguish
And the calm
Would fill,
That space my heart would then relinquish

…and eat it too

Look at us all grinning
On the glossy paper
Joyous faces beaming
Memories like no other
Eternity trapped in a moment
As if bottled up pure glee
A standstill, deepened second
Dust in the sun, floating free
Did we know at that time that we
Were saving cheer for a rainy day
When our heartsick minds would flee
Reality in pictures and albums and stray
From dismal Present to radiant Past
And we would Oh so regret not making it last
For we failed to taste that time's solace
While chasing a thrill too elusive to possess
And as we browse our lives, tearfully gazing upon
The nostalgic film of countless moments long gone
We wish we could, even once more
Embrace departed mates, hear voices we longed for
Pet lost companions, play youthful games
Sing olden songs, call forgotten names
In the silver memory brume dance the night away
For a glorious instant believe we maybe could stay
In that moment, and perhaps one last time make
A party of it and have some spongy birthday cake

Sometimes

Sometimes I lay awake
And even if my sheets are soft,
I can't help but notice
The rasping atmosphere I am coiled up in
Everything seems unfamiliar
As if hiding sinister intentions
And in the roughness of it all
Blooms a fear I can't explain
It soon seems to be coursing
Through my veins, dripping
From my forehead,
Oozing from my soul
It spills on the carpet, and I don't
Know how to wish it away
So, I try to wipe it
With a cloth at first but seeing
It persists, I bring a sponge and use
Circular motions in the hopes
That routine would absorb the spilled spleen
And I have to say that it
Usually works but, lately the sponge
Is so heavy I fear it
Won't contain the tears until
I first find a clear water where
I could wring it empty of all the despair…

Sky brushes

12

It was a perfect day
Sky flaking white clouds over blue
The birds floated, colorful array
Ivory, gray, onyx, all shades coming true
The vaporous firmament laid
An uncharted beryl baize
And the unflustered horizon made
A tranquil shore for the eye to gaze
Gently, a flighty sunrise
Shifted the soft undulating billow
Gold, coral, and mauve came in a trice
To adorn the first blush with their vibrant flow
Nature's splendid composition
Early morning's gifted display
Mending hearts, soothing disposition
It was a perfect day

Carousel

13

Monday brought its usual angst
Dripping uneasiness in a bitter coffee
Tuesday stretched a sharp tension
Through countless junctions and disputations alike
Wednesday's abating mid-week respite
Alleviated some of the denseness in lightsome caucus
Thursday dragged a humdrum series
Of stale numbers and toneless abstracts
Friday flourished in hopes of upcoming leisure
Gifting the lapsing work wings of earnestness
Saturday came bursting with spirited glee
Its reassuring warmth hatched myriad prospects
Sunday started a bit gray, uneager
Went quick…and swiftly, here comes Monday

Restlessness

Ever and again comes a time
No, a season when the mind,
Disquiet and flustered would
Devise the most distressing inferences
And trap all thoughts in a cruel snare
Where dolor and ruth reign supreme
The body in time would suffer
From the mind's bane and
Break into biting sweats, tremble,
Barely containing the throbbing heart
The wet palms might
Try to shelter the plagued face
Which tormented features could
Reflect that elusive part inside
Where its poison burgeoned
And then everything would seem
Removed, out of reach
Even that refuge one would invoke
When everything was drenched in weariness
Would come to naught in the presence
Of such uninhibited oppression
And often that scourge would
Last so long that
The exhausted being might
Give it frame to implore it
To let go at last but
Even if it did, the fear
Of it coming back for more,
Would leave body and mind
Restless…until dawn

When it happened…

Have you ever had
One of these moments when
Time stands still as if
The earth's rotation itself
Was disrupted by something
So awful that natural dynamics
Were affected and deranged
A moment when
All the air was sucked and
You stood in the vacuum
Struggling to inhale and then
Each breath would drop
As a stone in your stomach
Pushing you to the ground
A moment when
All the colors seemed
Vivid and menacing
And the most mundane object
Would threaten to detonate
Tearing your skin apart
In a cruel scarlet firework
A moment you feared so deeply
Just by instinct
That you wished you could leave your body
For a sturdier shell
Just to protect your soul from
The heartbreak threatening to wash away
Over it, as a salty sea wave
On raw vermilion skin

A moment when
Your frayed nerves screamed
While an eerie silence
Blossomed in your heart
Already mourning what was
And longing for your old self, the one before
The moment they tell you
And every fiber in your being
Vibrates in denial
And weeps in agony…
I did once and
Nothing was ever the same again
After that

Nana's kitchen

I find myself now and then
Yearning for a distant past
When I was a small bright-eyed child
With fistfuls of my Nana's clothing
I clung to her while she
Expertly hovered over the intimidating stove
That was covered in fuming pots and sizzling pans
The exquisite smells would
Leave their enticing aroma on my tongue
And before I could even taste the food
I grinned in utter enchantment
She would taste and season nimbly
Whipping colorful and fragrant spices
While the rich oriental musk
Filled the entire house, from
The dark blue zellige tiles to
The glittering crystal chandeliers
And we would all feel so full already
Full and content to be Home

How to enjoy a cup of tea

The water boiling is a waiting game
Where the mind can wander,
Where your eyes look inwards
Rummaging in knotted feelings
Use it to comb through all the oddities
And outlandish moods that originally
Called for a calming cup of hot tea
In a burning August afternoon
Then comes the pouring into the cup or mug
The scorching stream delicately cascades
In the vassal which must
Display a much pleasing scene
Of pastel colors, delicate greenery
Or the zesty message you need to empower that day
In bold vivid hues
Soon the dark shade of the tea
Spreads through the clear scalding water
And you pause to watch yourself, pensively
In the reflection and in reflection…
Adding the sugar is another game,
A guessing one where you
Gauge the white powder to
Decide how candied you want
Your calm afternoon to be
Before inhaling a big gulp
Of green/black/Grey tea
Because those aromatic fragrances
Might be heaven on earth, for the nerves
And the tasting! Oh, the tasting is

As if fulfilling the promise that delicious odor made
You feel the warmth making its way to your belly
And by some magic, it warms everything else
including
Your tiresome soul, your weary mind, untangles
Some of your worries
Gently nudges your fears and doubts
Until a hesitant smile flowers
If not on your face at least
Somewhere deep inside
And that is how you enjoy a cup of tea

Seasons

The leaves will sprout
Olive, willow, and lime
The leaves will sprout, in time

The leaves will darken
Amber, sepia, and brown
The leaves will darken, in time

The leaves will fall
Drop, tumble, and spill
The leaves will fall, in time

The leaves will fly
Float, flutter, and glide
The leaves will fly, in time